Living Logos

How Corporations Renew Their Image

David E. Carter

Editor

Art Direction Book Company
10 E. 39th Street
New York, NY 10016

Library of Congress Catalog Card Number: 92-074314
ISBN: 0-88108-107-8 Cloth
ISBN: 0-88108-108-6 Paper

Printed in Singapore

Contents

3M, 108

Ace Hardware Corporation, 22

Alpha Beta, 138

Aluminum Company of America, 28

American Express, 78

Ask Computer Systems, 98

Bank of America, 24

Baskin Robbins, 86

Best Products Co., 52

Betty Crocker, 148

British Airways, 44

Caterpillar, 58

Chase Manhattan Bank, 40

Chevron Corporation, 110

Chrysler Corporation, 132

Chubb Group of Insurance Companies, 132

CIGNA, 100

Citibank, 122

Coca-Cola, 8, 154, 156

Colt Industries, 48

Comerica Incorporated, 42

ConAgra, 88

Continental Airlines, 82

CSX Corporation, 152

Decathlon Corporation, 62

John Deere & Company, 10

Delta Air Lines, 30

Dole, 16

Eaton Corporation, 128

Garuda Indonesia, 50

General Electric Company, 126

The Great Atlantic & Pacific Tea Company, 72

Herman Miller Inc, 118

John Hancock Mutual Life Insurance Co., 116

Hilton Hotels, 54

Hyatt Hotels, 60

Japan Air Lines, 46

Learjet, 96

Libbey Owens Ford, 150

Moore Corporation, Ltd., 90

Motorola Inc., 12

Nalco Chemical Company, 94

Navistar International Corporation, 158

Norfolk Southern Corporation, 136

Northwest Airlines, 64

Oryx Energy Corporation, 142

Pepsi-Cola, 146

Phillips Petroleum Company, 56

Pizza Hut, 68

Primerica, 74

The Procter & Gamble Company, 124

The Prudential Insurance Company of America, 14

The Quaker Oats Company, 20

RCA, 66

Sears, Roebuck & Co., 114

Sovran Bank, 130

Sun Refining and Marketing Company, 140

Texaco, 26

Transamerica Corporation, 120

Trinova, 150

Trustmark, 70

United Airlines, 146

United Technologies, 76

Unocal Corporation, 112

US Air, 92

USX Corporation, 134

Western Union, 80

Westinghouse Corporation, 106

Xerox Corporation, 6

Zenith Electronics Corporation, 18

Acknowledgements

The editor wishes to express his appreciation to
all the companies who were kind enough to send
materials for this book, and for granting us
permission to have their logos included.

In addition, two of the world's leading corporate
identity consulting firms -- Landor Associates and
Lippincott & Margulies, Inc. -- should receive
special recognition. Each firm sent a large number
of "before and after" examples which appear in
this book.

Without the cooperation of all these firms, this
book could not have been produced.

Over a period of years, many companies have made changes in their logos. Some have been "evolutionary" steps which have maintained the equity of their previous design; others have been major visual re-structuring. And in some cases, a new corporate name created the need for a new system of corporate graphics.

This book addresses the issue of changes in corporate logos. The examples in this book cover a total of nearly 200 years, and some of the nation's best-known corporations are included. While the overall focus of the book is on American logos, a few international airlines are included since their examples are highly appropriate for this publication.

The book has many examples that can serve as a guide as companies and designers seek to maintain fresh and contemporary corporate identities.

1906

1948

1958

1961

1964

1967 (Current)

XEROX

The name Xerox, used as a logotype, is always shown in a single, specially designed letter form. This standard Xerox logotype, positioned within a horizontal identity stripe, is the only acceptable identification for the corporation and its organizations.

XEROX

XEROX

1876 Restored-1982

1912 Restored-1982

1936 Restored-1982

1937 Restored-1982

1950 Restored-1982

GALVIN MFG. CORPORATION

Motorola

Motorola

Motorola Inc.

Motorola Inc.

Motorola

Ʌ MOTOROLA

MOTOROLA INC.

1896

1900's

1920's

1940's

1950's

1970's

1977

1984

1877

1946

1957

QUAKER

1970

Historical Background

The name Ace was selected by the company's founders in a very straightforward, practical and functional manner as the name for a new hardware company. The company was organized in March 1928 as Ace Stores, Incorporated. Its logo, first used in 1929, was comprised of the word Ace with a biplane reversed out in a circle.

As the company grew in size and stature, the logo changed as well. The circular shape quickly gave way to a horizontal format, temporarily replacing the plane with two wings -- one inscribed with the word dependability; the other with the words and service. Between the wings were the words: Ace Stores Incorporated.

A year later in 1931 this logo changed to Ace Stores Inc. and incorporated a biplane against a winged background.

Even though the company changed its name from Ace Stores, Incorporated to Ace Hardware Corporation in September 1931, the logo remained basically the same with variations for several decades.

In the 1950s Ace Hardware, spelled out in one line, replaced Ace Stores.

The older plane was shelved for the contemporary jet in 1964. The wings were resized, and other modifications were made to modernize the logo.

One final change in design in the late 1960s introduced Ace Hardware in two lines within an inverted triangle. This basic design was registered and used until the new logo was introduced in May 1987.

A secondary version, called the slant log, was introduced in 1973. It reflects the slant of the polygon on the corporate logo. It soon came to represent Ace's private line of merchandise and programs.

1903

1907

1909

1915

1936

1963

1982

1894

1899

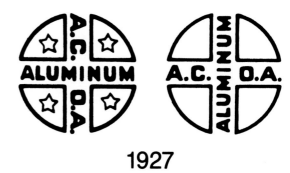

1927

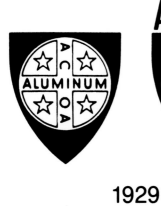

1929

1930

1943

1955

1963

33

1959
The Octagon Symbol was created as an architectural motif to accompany the newly built Chase Manhattan Plaza. It was designed by Chermayeff & Geismar Associates.

During this era, the names of Chase Units were represented in their full legal form, using these letterforms.

THE CHASE MANHATTAN BANK

1974
The Chase logotype was designed to compliment the octagon symbol. Their combination in several "lockups" formed the graphic foundation of a new corporate identity program created by Lefkowith Inc. The communicative name worldwide became "Chase."

1984
An interim identity program was undertaken to accommodate acquisitions and nationwide expansion.

1988
A simplified identity program was introduced to emphasize a uniform corporate identity for Chase. Graphic standards were tightened to produce more cohesive and cost-effective communications. The 1 o'clock lockup became the centerpiece of the identity program.

1991
Revised logo.

Detroit Bank & Trust changed its name to Comerica.

Comerica

FAIRBANKS WHITNEY

Fairbanks Whitney changed its name
to Colt Industries.

x

BEST™

HILTON
INTERNATIONAL

1927

1928

1930

1959

Hyatt Resots ℠

HYATT REGENCY ✿ MAUI ®

HYATT REGENCY ✿ WAIKOLOA ®

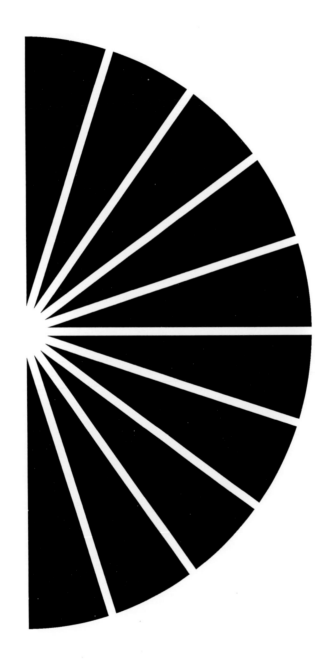

□ First National Bank

First National Bank changed
its name to Trustmark.

American Can

PRIMERICA

United
Aircraft

WESTERN UNION

Continental

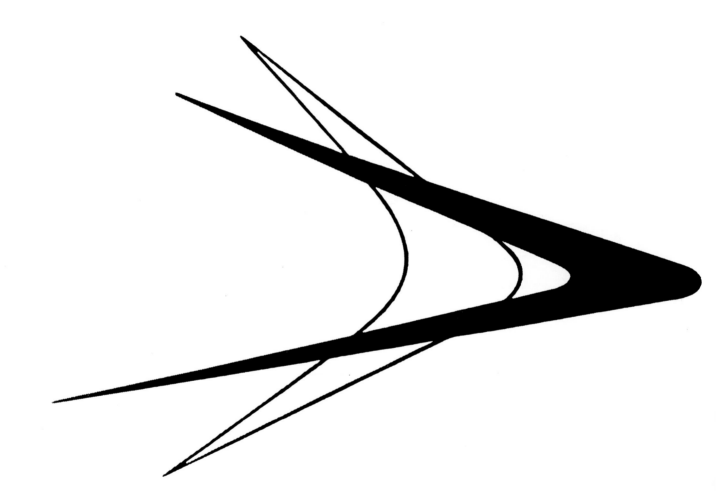

CHRYSLER

Baskin 31 Robbins

Nebraska Consolidated Mills

ConAgra

MOORE®

USAIR

USAir

SODIUM
NALCO
ALUMINATE

Nalco

Nalco

LEAR JET

GatesLearjet

Learjet

Connecticut General Life Insurance Company Logo used 1865 to about 1880.

CIGNA Corporation was formed in 1982 through a business combination effected by INA Corporation and Connecticut General Corporation. An INA subsidiary, the Insurance Company of North America, was formed in 1972 and a CG subsidiary, Connecticut General Life Insurance was formed in 1865. Both of the old insurance companies were the major operating subsidiaries of the combination partners and they remain important operating companies within CIGNA Corporation.

Special logo 1914

The "Connecticut General" service mark,
used from 1917 until the mid-1950s.

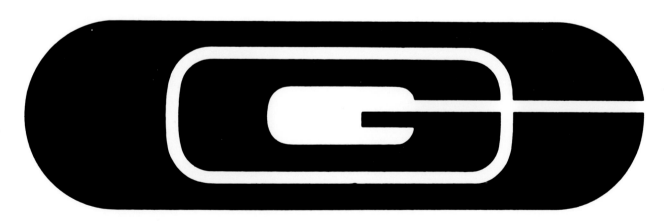

The modern CG logo, adopted 1956.

Insurance Company of North America
Seal of the Company, 1794.

The eagle firemark,
adopted 1795.

Revised eagle firemark,
about 1830.

A.

Eagle logo
about 1870.

INA Symbol/Logo
1957

1959

1973-1982

In 1982, Connecticut General and INA Corporations entered into a business combination, as a result of which they became subsidiaries of the newly formed CIGNA Corporation.

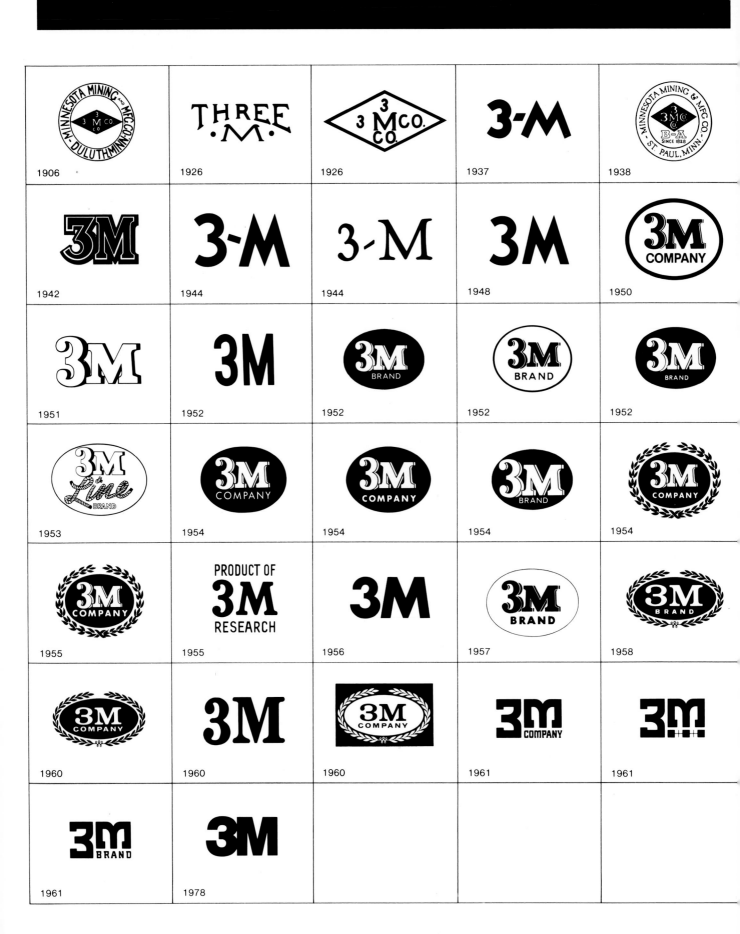

Chevron Corporation

UNOCAL 76

John Hancock MUTUAL LIFE INSURANCE COMPANY
BOSTON, MASSACHUSETTS

John Hancock

John Hancock®
companies

HERMAN MILLER
FURNITURE COMPANY

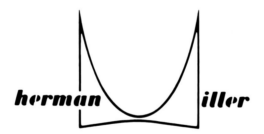

HERMAN MILLER INC
ZEELAND MICHIGAN

TRANSAMERICA

 **TRANSAMERICA**

HOW IT GREW

The crude cross, painted by a wharf hand on a wooden box of Star candles around 1851 was the beginning of the "Moon and Stars."

In time, the cross developed into this encircled star -- still merely part of the riverman's shipping "sign language."

The first standard trade-mark adopted by the company was this roughly drawn crescent enclosing thirteen stars.

The 1882 model "Moon and Stars" had been refined to this point, and registered in the U.S. Patent Office.

By 1902, our trade-mark, while basically the same, had taken on some of the "gingerbread" frills typical of the period.

Around 1920 came the return to effective simplicity -- still, however, with no fundamental change in the original design.

Finally, in 1930, a sculptor was commissioned by P&G to design this version of the famous "Moon and Stars."

Revised logo, 1991.

GENERAL  ELECTRIC

EATON

F&M

The new name was a result of a merger.

The company was formerly named US Steel.

SOUTHERN
THE RAILWAY SYSTEM THAT GIVES A GREEN LIGHT TO INNOVATIONS

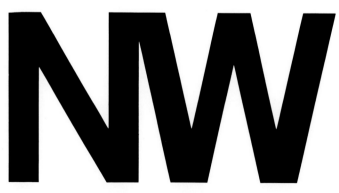

Norfolk and Western Railway Company

Norfolk Southern is a holding company for two railroads, each of which has been around more than 100 years.

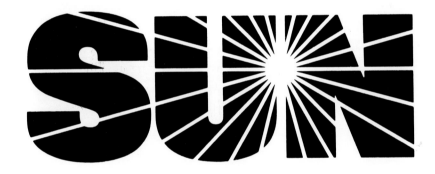

Oryx Energy was formerly a subsidiary of Sun Company and used the Sun logo before it assumed its separate identity.

ORYX

Oryx Energy Company

1898

1905

1906

1950

1936

1955

1965

1968

1972

1980

Used with the permission of General Mills, Inc.

In 1986, Libbey Owens Ford sold its LOF Glass Division to the Pilkington Group, along with the Libbey Owens Ford name. The company with the remaining divisions was kept intact and was re-named Trinova.

A member of the Pilkington Group

TRINOVA®

INTO THE 21ST CENTURY.®

The Coca-Cola bottles from 1894 through 1975 are shown left to right.

1. Hutchinson-Style Bottle: Type unit in which Coca-Cola was first bottled in 1894 by Joseph A. Biedenharn, Vicksburg, Mississippi -- the first bottler of Coca-Cola.

2. Hutchinson-Style Bottle used 1899-1902: This style was used briefly by Bottlers of Coca-Cola after Novémber 1899 and before 1903.

3 and 4. Straight-sided bottle with the trade-mark Coca-Cola embossed in glass: Type unit designed for crown closures and distributed with the diamond-shaped label between 1900-1916, inclusive. Both flint and amber bottles were used by the bottlers of Coca-Cola during this period.

5. The first glass package for Coca-Cola using classic contour design and introduced into the market in 1916.

6 and 7. Two successive designs with patent revisions used between 1923 and 1951 when the 1937 patent expired. In 1960, the contour design for the bottle was registered as a trademark.

8. Applied Color Label, for trade-mark Coca-Cola on panels, introduced on all sizes of classic contour bottles for Coca-Cola in 1957 and continued thereafter.

9. The no-return, or one-way glass bottle, first introduced in 1961; later modified for twist-top.

10. Experimental plastic 10-oz. package for Coca-Cola classic contour design with twist-top cap; tested, 1970-1975. This package was not in general circulation; spring, 1975.

The International Harvester Company sold the International Harvester name and the familiar IH logo, but maintained "International" as a brand name under the new corporate name of Navistar.

American Corporate Identity (7 volumes)
Corporate Identity Manuals
Designing Corporate Identity Programs
        for Small Companies
Evolution of Design
Logos of America's Largest Corporations
Logos of Major World Corporations
Logos of America's Fastest-Growing Companies
World Corporate Identity (2 volumes)
Book of American Trade Marks (11 volumes)
How to Improve Your Corporate Identity
Designing Corporate Symbols
Logo International (4 volumes)
Letterheads (7 volumes)
Trends in Logos